Protecting Habitats

Mountains
in Danger

Robert Snedden

W
FRANKLIN WATTS
LONDON•SYDNEY

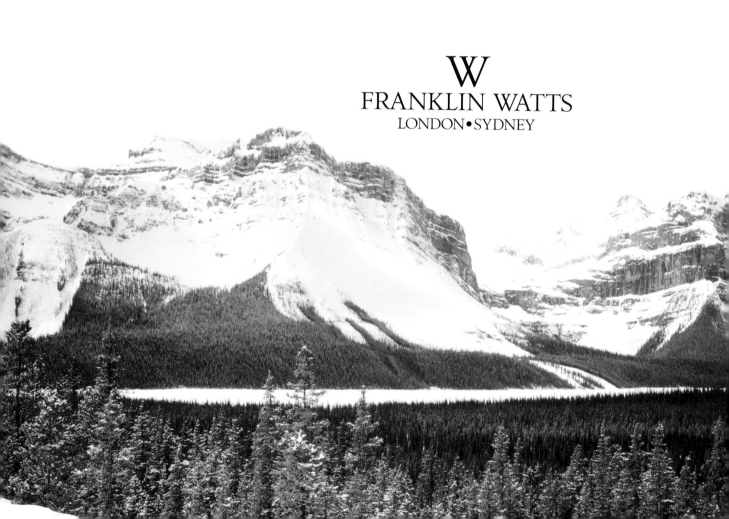

Designer Rita Storey
Editor Sarah Ridley
Art Director Jonathan Hair
Editor-in-Chief John C. Miles
Picture Research Susan Mennell

© 2005 Franklin Watts

First published in 2005
by Franklin Watts
96 Leonard Street
London
EC2A 4XD

Franklin Watts Australia
45-51 Huntley Street
Alexandria
NSW 2015

ISBN 0 7496 5820 7

A CIP catalogue record for this book is
available from the British Library.

Printed in China

Picture Credits
Cover images: Ecoscene

Ecoscene: pp. 1 (Anthony Cooper), 4
(Anthony Cooper), 9 (Robert Weight),
12 (Promeck Services), 13 (Paul Thompson),
22 (Sally Morgan), 24 (Fritz Polking)
Oxford Scientific Films: pp. 16 (Mark Jones),
23 (Mary Plage), 26 (Stephen Miller)
Photolibrary.com: p. 21
Still Pictures: pp. 5 (Jeremy Woodhouse),
8 (Jeremy Woodhouse), 10 (Markus Dlouhy),
14 (M & C Denis-Huot), 17 (M. Boulton),
19 (Joerg Boethling), 20 (Knut Mueller),
25 (F. Suchel)

Every attempt has been made to clear copyright.
Should there be any inadvertent omission, please
apply to the publisher for rectification.

Note to parents and teachers
Every effort has been made by the Publishers to ensure that the
websites in this book are suitable for children, that they are of the
highest educational value, and that they contain no
inappropriate or offensive material. However, because of the
nature of the Internet, it is impossible to guarantee that the
contents of these sites will not be altered. We strongly advise that
Internet access is supervised by a responsible adult.

CONTENTS

All about mountains

Mountains have always fascinated people. Their remoteness and beauty are inspiring. Until adventurers and explorers went up to take a look, many people believed that mountains were the home of the gods.

Today, mountains are under threat. Ski lifts scar the mountainsides. Farmers drive their herds high into the alpine meadows to graze, eroding the soil and threatening the fragile ecosystem. Less visible, but no less serious, global warming pushes mountain plants and animals towards extinction as they struggle to escape its effects.

Shaping the world

Mountains shape the land around them in many ways. They affect the weather, blocking rainfall so that the land in the

A photograph of part of the Rocky Mountains in winter at Banff, Alberta, Canada.

ISLAND REFUGES

A mountain stands out in the landscape like an island in the middle of an ocean. These are places where animals, as well as humans, have found refuge from the pressures of living in the lowlands. Species driven out by human activity in the lowlands may survive here.

Mountains have been described as "islands of biodiversity" because there is a huge variety of plants and animals living there that are quite different to those found in the surrounding lowlands. In the mountains there are living things found nowhere else in the world.

shadow of a mountain range can become a parched desert. Mountains can also give water to the land, as the melting snow and ice from their peaks run down to feed rivers that lead from mountain ranges to the sea.

Mountains have also played their part in shaping history. Their huge size and sheer slopes formed impassable barriers to all but the most determined invaders and explorers. Many mountain ranges continue to mark the geographical boundaries between one

country and another. A town or village in the mountains has ready-made natural defences and for centuries the very remoteness of mountains has made them places of refuge for people fleeing from persecution elsewhere.

Today aircraft fly over mountain ranges, and road and rail links tunnel through them. Although people can now cross mountains, they remain extraordinary features of our landscape.

The mighty Andes mountains run the length of South America. Here, vicuña graze near salt pans in the Altiplano region of Chile.

Where to find mountains

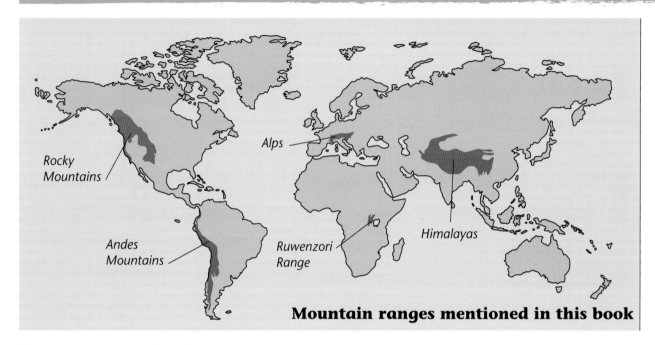

Mountain ranges mentioned in this book

Rocky Mountains

Alps

Andes Mountains

Ruwenzori Range

Himalayas

There are mountains in every continent in the world. They cover around a fifth of the Earth's land surface and there are many more hidden from sight beneath the ocean. Most mountains lie in groups called ranges, each with their own characteristic plants and wildlife.

The Himalayas

Himalaya means "house of the snow". More than twenty of the world's tallest mountains are here, including Mount Everest, at 8,848 m (29,020 ft). The Himalayan mountain chain stretches for 2,400 km (1,500 miles), crossing the countries of Bhutan, Nepal, Tibet, India and Pakistan.

On the lower Himalayan slopes – up to about 2,000 m (6,600 ft) or so above sea level – chestnut trees, laurels and oaks grow. Tea plants and rhododendron bushes are also common. Pine trees and other conifers grow on the higher slopes up to around 3,500 m (11,500 ft).

The lower slopes of the southern Himalayas support tropical forest, which contains tigers, monkeys and Asian elephants. Higher up live animals such as the yak.

The Rocky Mountains

The Rocky Mountains run like a backbone down nearly 5,000 km (3,100 miles) of North America, from Alaska in the north, down to New Mexico in the south. The tallest peak is Mount McKinley at 6,194 m (20,000 ft). The Missouri, the Columbia and the Rio Grande rivers all begin in the Rockies. Because the Rockies run so far north to south they stretch across a number of climate zones and are home to a wide range of plants and animals.

The Andes

The Andes mountain range is the longest in the world and also has some of the highest

MOUNTAIN BUILDING

The surface of our planet is never still. The seemingly solid crust of the Earth is made up of enormous slow-moving segments called plates. Where two plates collide they buckle up, forming huge mountain ranges. The growth of a mountain range is not something that happens quickly. The Himalayas, for example, were born when the plate carrying India collided with the plate carrying part of Asia (see diagram at right). Fifty million years later the mountains of the Himalayas are still growing by around 1 cm every year.

Mountains can also be formed when molten rock beneath the surface forces its way up through a weakness in the crust, forming a volcano. The tallest mountain in Africa, Kilimanjaro, is a volcano, and so too is the world's tallest mountain, Mauna Kea, in the Hawaiian Islands. Mauna Kea is over 10,000 m (32,800 ft) tall, but the lower 6,000 m (19,680 ft) is hidden beneath the Pacific Ocean.

This diagram shows the stages by which the Indian plate collided with the Asian plate millions of years ago, creating the Himalayas.

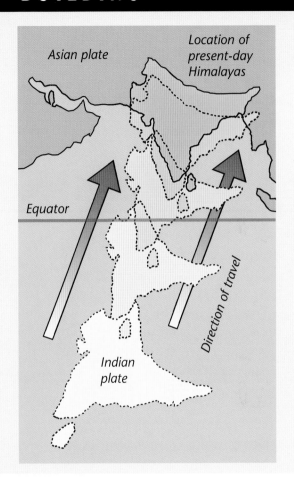

mountains, with Mount Aconcagua at 6,960 m (22,830 ft) the tallest in the range. The Andes run for more than 7,200 km (4,500 miles) along the western edge of South America from Panama to Cape Horn at the tip of Chile. Like the Rockies, the Andes span a range of climates.

The Ruwenzori range
The small Ruwenzori range is located in eastern Africa, on the border that runs between Uganda and the Democratic Republic of Congo. It is about 120 km (75 miles) long and 65 km (40 miles) wide. The highest peak in the range soars to 5,109 m (16,761 ft) and is permanently snow-capped. Along with the isolated

Mount Kilimanjaro and Mount Kenya, these are the only snow-capped mountains in Africa.

The Alps
The Alps are the largest mountain range in Europe, stretching in a 1,000-km (620-mile) curve from southern Germany and Austria, down through Switzerland, southern France and northern Italy almost to the Mediterranean Sea. The highest peak, Mont Blanc, lies between France, Italy and Switzerland and is over 4,800 m (15,750 ft) high. The name Alps comes from the Latin meaning "high mountains" and that is why high-altitude habitats around the world are referred to as "alpine" habitats.

Mountain science

Conditions on a mountain can change rapidly, making it a challenging environment for the plants and animals that live there.

Take a deep breath

If you climb high into hills or mountains, or go skiing, it might not be simply lack of fitness that makes you breathe more heavily. One very important factor that mountain climbers have to consider is that the higher you climb the thinner the air becomes, and the less essential oxygen there is available to breathe. Most of the climbers who have made it to the top of Mount Everest have taken oxygen cylinders and breathing equipment with them, though a few have managed without.

Animals that live at high altitudes not only have larger lungs than low-altitude animals but also have around three times as many of the red blood cells that are responsible for carrying oxygen from the lungs to the rest of the body. People who live at high altitudes, such as the Sherpas of the Himalayas and the people of the Andes, are similarly adapted. Animals that move up and down the slopes over the course of the year make adjustments to their red-blood cell count, making more red blood cells as they move back up to higher altitudes. Human mountain climbers and competitive skiers can also become acclimatized to high altitudes in this way.

Temperature drop

Not only does the air get thinner at high altitude, but the temperature drops also. For every 100 m (330 ft) climbed the temperature will drop by between 0.6 and 1°C, depending on how dry the air is. It is these low temperatures that explain why mountain peaks are often covered in snow.

The atmosphere becomes much thinner and colder at high altitudes. This photograph shows part of Grand Teton National Park in Wyoming, USA.

Above a certain point, called the snowline, the temperature falls below freezing. The height of the snowline will depend on where in the world the mountain is situated. A mountain in the tropics, where the surrounding climate is warm, will have a high snowline, perhaps over 4,000 m (13,000 ft) up. A mountain in the polar regions, with low temperatures year-round, will be almost entirely snow-covered. High winds at the top of a mountain can make it feel very cold indeed.

Conditions on a mountain in the tropics can be rather odd. High up on the mountain the air is clear so the sun can warm the ground very quickly through the thin blanket of air. However, thin air is no good at trapping heat and as soon as the sun disappears the temperature plummets again.

RADIATION HAZARD

Another high-altitude hazard comes from ultraviolet (UV) radiation from the sun. At lower levels the atmosphere blocks out much of this harmful radiation, although enough gets through to damage unprotected skin in the summer. In response, mountain animals are often dark in colour, as the black pigment absorbs the harmful UV rays and helps to prevent damage to the animal. UV rays are also very harmful to the eyes which is one of the reasons why mountaineers, such as the one shown below, wear protective goggles.

Water and weather

The influence of mountains on the areas around them is huge. Half the people in the world rely on rivers fed by mountain streams. The mountains store water in the form of snow and ice that thaws and feeds the rivers in spring. Mountains also have a big effect on the weather patterns of lower-lying areas.

World watertowers

Snow falling on mountaintops doesn't melt because it is so cold there. Year after year, snow builds up and the weight compresses the lower layers into ice, forming a glacier. A glacier is like a giant river of ice that flows slowly down the mountainside. Eventually, the lower tongue of the glacier moves down past the snowline where the temperature rises above freezing. Here it begins to melt, creating streams that feed into rivers, bringing vital fresh water to the lowlands surrounding the mountain range. Because mountain streams are fed from the frozen glacier reservoirs, rivers with their sources in high mountain ranges continue to flow, even in times of drought.

Weather patterns

Airflow hitting a mountain is forced upwards. As it rises, the air cools and any moisture carried in it will condense and fall as rain or snow. The land on the windward side of the mountain benefits from this rainfall, and the slopes on this side may be densely forested. On the other side of the mountain, however, things may be quite different. By the time the clouds have moved over the mountain, they have a lot less moisture in them. Additionally, as the air moves down the mountain it warms up, so any moisture left in it is less likely to fall as rain. The land on the dry side of the mountain is said to be in a rainshadow.

The Andes mountain range shelters the Atacama Desert so effectively that in some places it hasn't rained for hundreds of years! The grassy steppes of northern Asia are kept dry by the Urals to the west and the Altai mountains to the south. The mountains are also the reason why Siberian winters are so cold – they trap freezing air flowing in from the Arctic.

THE WIND FROM THE MOUNTAINS

The cold, dense air at the top of a mountain doesn't just sit there. Gravity pulls it back down the mountain, blowing it into the lowlands below as wind. Mountain valleys and gullies can strengthen and focus the wind, causing it to blow harder.

One such wind is the mistral, which blows down from the Alps, across southern France and over the Mediterranean at speeds that can reach around 100 km/h (60 mph).

Another mountain wind is the chinook, or Snow Eater, of North America. As the air sinks down from the Rocky Mountains it is compressed and gets warmer. Often arising after an intensely cold spell of weather, the chinook can cause rapid localised warming.

Melting ice and snow can produce spectacular
mountain waterfalls, such as this one in Iceland.

Mountain zones

From the heat of the tropics around the equator to the frozen wastelands of the polar regions in the far north and south, the world is divided into a number of climate zones. Going up a mountain is a little like travelling through a series of changing climate zones piled one above another within the space of a few hundred metres.

The zones

Just like world climate zones, mountain zones are divided according to the type of plants that live there. These have adapted to the changing conditions found at increasing altitudes. The climber ascends through a number of different biomes, meaning continuous stretches of natural habitat. So you move through broad-leaved forest at the bottom of the mountain, passing in to evergreen forest, grassland and tundra, to reach the alpine biome just beneath the snowline. Higher than this, on the mountain equivalent of the polar icecaps, very little can survive on the bare rocks and snowfields of the high peaks.

A mountain in a temperate climate zone will have warm summers and cool winters, just as there are in the surrounding landscape. These conditions suit broad-leaved trees that shed their leaves in the winter, and the lower slopes of a mountain may be thickly forested.

Meadows on the upper slopes of mountain ranges are filled with flowers in summer. Here, globe buttercups flourish in the Alps.

SPECIAL CONDITIONS

As you travel north or south from the equator in wintertime the length of the days gets shorter. From top to bottom of a mountain, however, the length of day is just the same. This creates some interesting conditions for plants living in mountain habitats. At the top of a mountain it is cold all the time, but the plants living there get as much sunlight as those on the lowest slopes. This means that mountaintop plants are very different to those of, for example, the Arctic, which have had to adapt to both cold and lack of light in winter.

Needle-bearing trees called conifers are adapted to survive in snowy conditions, as shown in this photograph taken near Soll in Austria.

Further up the mountain conditions are cooler. Broadleaved trees like the oak cannot survive here. Conifers, trees that are better suited to low temperatures, become more numerous on the higher slopes, just as they are in the northern forests.

The treeline

Even the well-adapted conifers cannot survive right the way up the mountain. Above a certain height the conditions become so harsh that no tree can grow. This height is called the treeline. Above the treeline, there are other, smaller plants. This zone is called the alpine meadow and in spring it can be covered in a dazzling display of flowers.

Higher than the alpine meadows on the highest mountains are bare rocks where tough lichens might be present (see pg 15). Higher still, above the snowline, no plants live in the frozen icefields. However, there are survivors even here. Just under the surface of the snow live microscopic single-celled algae.

Mountain plants

Some mountain plants appear strange, but are adapted to survive in highland conditions. This giant senecon is from the Ruwenzori range in Africa.

Mountain plants have developed different ways of surviving according to how high up the mountain they live. At the foot of the mountain vegetation, such as dense broad-leaved forest, will be much the same as it is in surrounding lowland areas. As you ascend the slopes, this gives way to plants better adapted to living at higher altitudes.

Mountain conifers

Conifers have dark green leaves that they keep throughout the year. Dark leaves absorb heat from the sun more quickly than light-coloured leaves do, and warm leaves make food faster than cold ones. By keeping its leaves year-round the tree is ready to make food whenever the sun appears and to do so efficiently. The cone shape of a conifer is another adaptation to high-altitude life. As the temperature falls higher up the mountain there is a greater likelihood of snow falling. Because of the tree's shape, most snow that settles on the conifer will slide off without damaging its branches. Conifers also have shallow root systems that spread out widely in the thin soil.

Alpine meadows

Alpine plants are brightly coloured to attract the few insect pollinators that live there. At higher altitudes still, the soil cover becomes even thinner and the bare rock of the mountain-top is exposed. A few species of plant are able to take root in little pockets of soil trapped between the rocks. These high-altitude plants often have dark leaves to absorb as much heat as possible from the sun, and hairy surfaces to act as a blanket holding on to the little warmth that is available. Alpine plants are much smaller than plants at lower altitudes. Tall plants would be torn apart by the winds.

High-altitude team

The only plants that grow on the bare mountain rocks are lichens. A lichen isn't a flowering plant. It is actually a partnership between simple plants called algae and a fungus. The fungus grips the rock surface, producing chemicals that dissolve the rock surface, and the algae make food from sunlight for both to share. It takes teamwork to survive in the high mountains. Lichens are extremely slow-growing, spreading only a few centimetres over decades.

ONE POTATO, TWO POTATO...

Around twenty plant varieties supply 80% of the food eaten by the human race. Six of them – maize, barley, sorghum, apples, tomatoes and potatoes – were first discovered in mountain areas. The Andes are the home of the potato, one of the world's most important vegetable crops. The wild potato was discovered growing in the mountains by people living in what is now the country of Peru and it was first grown as a crop about 4,500 years ago. Andean farmers know of more than 200 different varieties of potato growing in the mountains. Wild potatoes will grow where the climate is too cold for other staple crops, such as wheat or corn.

Mountain animals

Mountainous regions are difficult places in which to survive, and animals living there face a range of weather conditions. Indeed, the highest mountain environment is similar in some ways to that of the Earth's polar regions, although obviously there are differences. One big difference, mentioned earlier, is that the air grows thinner at high altitude; mountain animals have adapted to make maximum use of such oxygen as is available.

Keeping warm

Another obvious problem faced by mountain animals is the cold. Only warm-blooded animals can survive in the highest reaches of the mountains. Although some reptiles and amphibians are found as high up as the coniferous forests, there are none in the high mountain regions. These cold-blooded creatures rely on the warmth of the sun and there just isn't enough of it for them to survive up there. They also lack anything in the way of insulating fur or feathers.

HIGH-FLYING BIRDS

Several types of bird are found in mountains, including some of the most spectacular in the world. The Andes, for example, are home to both the mighty Andean condor, one of the world's biggest and rarest birds of prey, and the world's highest altitude hummingbirds, such as the Estella hummingbird, which can be found living nearly 5,000 m (16,400 ft) up.

Hikers in the mountains of Canada often find their campsites being visited by whiskey-jacks. These bold jays will quickly snatch away any unattended morsels of food.

The Andean condor's huge wings are adapted for riding the warm air currents found in the Andes.

The wild yak's thick, hairy coat protects it from biting Himalayan winds.

Alpine animals have adapted to the cold in a number of ways. Some, such as the black bears of the Rocky Mountain forests, escape the worst of the winter cold by going into hibernation in a warm secure den until conditions improve in the spring. Other animals leave the higher parts of the mountain and migrate downwards to the warmer lower slopes in the winter.

Animals such as mountain goats follow the snowline as it moves up and down with the changing seasons. As the retreating snow exposes the soil the goats dig up the roots and bulbs of alpine plants. The yak is the highest-altitude mountain mammal; it manages to feed on lichens scraped from rocks 6,000 m (20,000 ft) up in the Himalayas.

Most mountain mammals are protected from the cold by thick, furry coats and layers of insulating fat. The body shape of a mountain animal may also be different from that of its lowland relatives. Its legs, tail and ears are likely to be shorter – all adaptations to reduce the loss of heat.

Get a grip!
Mountain animals also have to be agile enough to make their way across difficult terrain. The Himalayan yak, for instance, has short legs and broad hooves with large dew-claws on the inside leg that help it to grip the often treacherous surfaces of its mountain habitat. The Rocky Mountain bighorn sheep keeps a sure-footed grip on steep mountain slopes with its soft and flexible hooves.

Mountain people

Mountains are challenging environments for people to live in, but though it's tough to make a living in the mountains, many people around the world still manage to do so. About a tenth of the world's population – roughly 600 million people – live in mountainous regions. Half of them live in the Himalayas, the Andes and the mountain ranges of Africa.

Survival skills

Mountain people often live in conditions that would seem harsh to most of us. In developing countries in particular, many mountain people live as nomads, hunters and gatherers, traders, small farmers and herders. Because their lives depend on being knowledgeable about their environment, mountain people have built up a wealth of experience of the mountains and their plants and animals.

On pages 25-27 you can see how this knowledge can help everyone on Earth to protect the mountain environment.

Sherpas

Among the most famous of the mountain peoples are the Sherpas of the Himalayas. Around 35,000 to 40,000 Sherpas live in the mountains of Nepal and some also live in India, Bhutan and Tibet. For centuries the Sherpas have lived here as farmers, yak herders and traders. These tough, resourceful people have a phenomenal reputation as climbers. In 1953 Tenzing Norgay Sherpa, along with New Zealander Sir Edmund Hillary, became the first to reach the summit of Mount Everest. Today a significant number of Sherpas earn their living from guiding climbers in the Himalayas (see pg 20). Some people are concerned that the lifestyle of the Sherpas is being changed by their increasing dependence on tourist money.

People of the Altiplano

The Altiplano, or high plains, lie between the forests of the Amazon and the peaks of the Andes. It is a harsh environment of poor soils, wide variations in temperature, little plant or animal life and lies at an average

WORKING IN HARMONY

Mountain valleys often have fine fertile soils and may also be sheltered and warm. If it were not for the steep slopes they would be ideal for farming. To adapt to these conditions people in many parts of the world, particularly in South-east Asia, have shaped the lower mountain slopes into a series of flat terraces that run around the hillside. Important food crops, such as rice, have been produced in terraced farms for many centuries. Terracing is a good example of people working in harmony with the mountain environment. The terraces are walled to keep in water and prevent the soil from being washed downhill. Other forms of agriculture in which the ground is simply ploughed up or grazed by animals may cause erosion, as the soil is loosened and washes away, with consequent habitat loss.

height of 4,000 m (13,000 ft) above sea level. Yet it is here that the peoples of the Andes, mainly Aymara and Quechua Indians, make their living. The Andean people have become adapted to high-altitude life. Their hearts and lungs are bigger than those of most lowlanders, helping them to cope with the lack of oxygen. An important crop here is the potato, some varieties of which can be grown as high as 4,500 m (15,000 ft) up. Herds of alpaca and llamas are also kept, feeding on the tough grasses that grow as high as the frost deserts at 5,000 m (16,500 ft).

Two traditionally dressed Sherpa women from the Himalayas spin yarn from plant fibres.

Mountains in danger

Mountains look solid and unchanging and mountain habitats can seem remote and safe from human interference. Sadly, they are not. Threats to the mountain environment are increasing all the time.

Population pressure

Farmers in many parts of the world find themselves under increasing pressure to find more land on which to grow crops to feed a growing, hungry population. The mountain habitats of Africa in particular are being hard hit. Almost half of the mountain regions of Africa are now farmed in some way, with a third of the mountain habitat grazed by animals. The pressure of the animals' hooves breaks up the fragile mountain soil, causing erosion. At the same time the animals consume the very plants that help hold the soil together.

The tourist toll

For many people of the world's wealthier nations the mountains have become something of a playground. Modern means of transport are making regions that were once very difficult to reach accessible to practically anyone who can afford to go there. Around 70 million people around the world enjoy winter sports, but their pleasure can put pressure on fragile environments.

In 1964 20 trekkers from other parts of the world arrived in the Everest region of Nepal. By 2000 their numbers had increased to 27,000. Four-fifths of households in the region get a major part of their income from tourism. The number of trekkers is taking a severe toll on the mountain environment. It is estimated that around 17 tons of rubbish left behind by trekkers are strewn along every kilometre of the Everest trail.

Many African mountain regions have been cleared for farming and grazing.

TOURIST ATTRACTION

Tourists bring money with them, and that money attracts people keen to offer services that tourists will pay for. In the Alps, for example, many families are moving from small farming communities to live and work around a handful of large tourist resorts. The effect of this can be an increase in soil erosion in the abandoned farming areas. This is because traditional methods of farming help to anchor the soil and keep it healthy. When the farmers depart, the untended soil is exposed to the full harshness of the mountain climate.

Downhill disasters

The popularity of skiing holidays, particularly in the mountains of Europe and North America, puts huge pressure on the mountain environment. This comes not only from the building of chalets, skilifts and cable cars that scar the hillsides, but also from the pollution from the exhausts of the countless vehicles ferrying skiers and their equipment up and down the mountainside. The use of offroad vehicles and snowmobiles also causes damage to the slopes. However, as we shall see on the next spread, changes in the world's climate could eventually force many ski resorts to close.

The popularity of ski resorts and tourism has put enormous pressure on fragile mountain habitats.

Mountains and climate change

There are many who believe that human activities are altering the world's climates by causing global temperatures to rise. Burning fossil fuels, such as oil and coal, releases carbon dioxide into the atmosphere. Increasing levels of carbon dioxide acts like a greenhouse, preventing the heat from escaping into space. Mountain habitats and the plants and animals that live there are particularly vulnerable to this warming effect.

Moving mountain zones

No one can be quite sure what effect global warming might have on mountain habitats but already changes can be observed. The rise in global temperatures may be felt all through the mountain habitat zones. According to some researchers a rise in the world's temperature of three degrees or so will shift the mountain climate zones upwards by about 500 m (1,640 ft). A study in Norway found that many plants had moved up to 300 m (980 ft) higher in the last sixty years. For those plants and animals at the top of the mountain ranges there just won't be anywhere left to go.

Global warming may be causing glaciers, such as this one in Alberta, Canada, to melt.

SKIING GOES DOWNHILL

The loss of snow cover on the mountains would have a catastrophic effect on those mountain communities that depend on skiing and other winter sports for their income. As global warming pushes the snowline ever higher many ski resorts will find themselves without any reliable snowfall. Avalanches from above would be hazardous for skiers.

If the snowfields vanish all that would be left is bare rock with no soil for the alpine meadow plants to colonize. Meanwhile, the expanding conifer forests would threaten the alpine meadow plants as the upper limit of the treeline grew higher. At the same time, of course, the broad-leaf forest would be pushing from below into the conifers.

Some of the world's rarest wildlife is at severe risk. Animals, such as the Tibetan yak, are so well adapted to cold conditions that they will find it hard to survive when their homes disappear. In Australia the mountain pygmy possum is likely to become extinct if average temperatures rise a single degree.

Shrinking glaciers

In practically every mountain range in the world, from Greenland to the Rockies to the Alps and the Andes, icefields and glaciers are shrinking at an alarming rate. Glaciers in the Alps are only half as big as they were a century ago. If current trends continue, by the end of this century Glacier National Park in the Rocky Mountains will have to be renamed – there won't be any glaciers left!

The disappearance of glaciers will have a huge effect. The exposed tops of the mountains will be liable to erosion, increasing the likelihood of rockslides and avalanches that could cause damage on the lower slopes. The mountain streams and rivers fed by the glaciers will first flood as the ice and snow melts, and will then gradually begin to dry up as their water source is lost.

The yak is one of many mountain animals that are under threat worldwide.

Saving mountain wildlife

Mountain wildlife is hardy and well-adjusted to its often harsh habitat. The plants and animals of the mountains are in balance with their habitat. If their habitat is damaged, that balance is lost.

Year of the Mountains

Mountains were once seen as environmental "poor relations" compared to the oceans and the rainforests. There was plenty of publicity for saving rainforest animals and whales and dolphins, but not much for the

One of the most severely endangered animals in the word is the mountain gorilla, which lives in the mist-covered highlands of Central Africa.

PROTECTED MOUNTAINS

Many mountain areas around the world are protected by law as nature reserves or national parks. Greenland National Park (below), established in 1974, is the largest protected area in the world and covers an area larger than Britain and France put together. Even so, less than a tenth of the world's mountain habitats enjoy any sort of protection.

alpine meadows. In fact, although rainforest destruction is widely, and rightly, condemned, the forests that are disappearing fastest are the cloud forests on the slopes of the Andes and the tropical mountains of Africa and South-east Asia.

In 2002 an attempt was made to change that when the International Year of Mountains was celebrated. By July 2004, forty countries, from Afghanistan to Venezuela, and organizations such as the World Bank, UNESCO and the World Wildlife Fund had joined together to form the Mountain Partnership. Their aim is to protect mountain habitats and improve the lives of mountain people.

Local skills

Mountain people know better than anyone what is being lost when the fragile mountain environment is damaged. A few years ago in the Indian Himalayas national foresters listed 25 different types of plants that had been destroyed by logging and mining operations in the area. Local mountain women could actually identify 145 types of plants lost to the miners and loggers.

In most cases mountain people do not own the land they live on. Laws that give mountain communities the right to decide what happens to their homes would be a big step forward in helping to preserve the mountain environment. Mountain people know, for example, that in a habitat as varied as the mountains, traditional sheep and goat farming and small-scale agriculture work best. In the mountains of Nepal, for instance, 2,000 varieties of rice are grown. Replacing this traditionally diverse approach by ploughing up the land, introducing single-crop cultivation or driving herds of cows up on to the alpine meadows, could be disastrous.

Collecting knowledge

Perhaps because they are so inaccessible mountains are one of the least studied natural habitats, but if we are to preserve the mountain habitat we have to understand how it works. As we have seen the native peoples of the mountains have a great storehouse of knowledge that we can draw on. We can also use modern advances in technology such as radio tracking devices to monitor the movements of animals across the mountains and record their numbers.

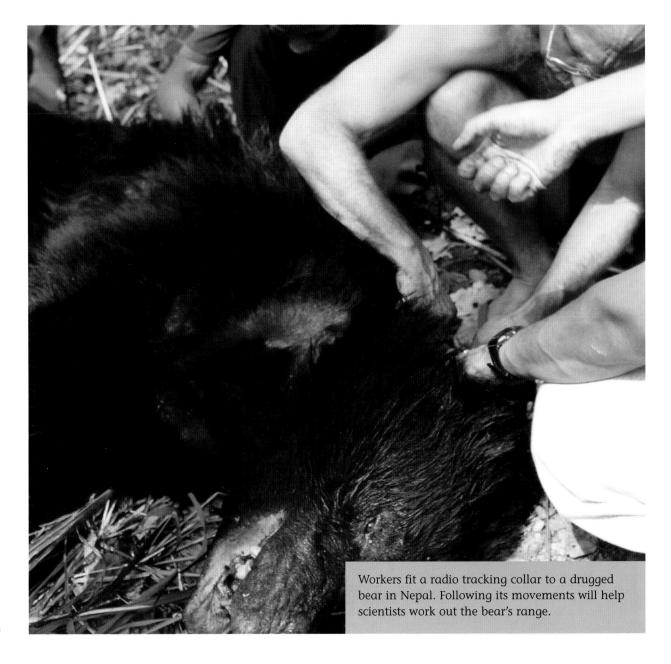

Workers fit a radio tracking collar to a drugged bear in Nepal. Following its movements will help scientists work out the bear's range.

MOUNTAIN WOMEN

"If you want to know, ask the women." Researchers studying mountain farming techniques often find themselves directed to women if they have questions about seeds and plants. It is the women of the mountain peoples who hold most of the knowledge regarding biodiversity in the mountains. They need to have this knowledge because it is usually the women who plant the crops, make remedies from plants and herbs, and manage the household. Crop failure can mean starvation and disaster. Women are involved at every stage of the process, from planting seeds to harvesting and preparing the crop. They know how to protect the plants from pests, and which varieties grow best.

The view from above

Global Land Ice Measurement from Space (GLIMS) is a project that was designed to monitor the world's glaciers by observing them from space. Monitoring the glaciers provides a sensitive early indication of changes in the world brought about by global warming. At the moment the signs are not good. All over the world the glaciers are shrinking. Satellite images also reveal the extent of the damage done to mountain forests by extensive logging.

Satellite tracking systems using global positioning technology (GPS) can actually allow researchers to keep track of single animals moving in their mountain home. First, of course, the animal has to be safely captured, collared with the tracking device and then released unharmed back into the wild. This may be no simple task if the animal in question is a 100-kg (220-lb) mountain lion! Using the tracking devices researchers can, for example, track a herd of mountain goats to find out what their grazing patterns are.

Knowing the range of the animals is of great importance in marking out areas as wildlife refuges.

Measuring diversity

Biodiversity means the variety of living things. Keeping that diversity high is vital to the health of the planet. The greater the diversity in a habitat the more different forms of life it supports. Diversity shows the links between living things. If there is a great variety of plants in an area there is likely to be a great variety of insects living on them, and the insects will, in turn, attract a variety of birds to eat them.

The mountains may not be thought of as being as rich in diversity as the rainforests or the oceans, but within the differing zones of a mountain range such as the Rocky Mountains there can be over 10,000 different species of plants and animals. There are so many different smaller habitats within the large mountain habitat that the mountains are often richer in plants and animals than elsewhere. As we have also seen, there are plants and animals on the mountains that are found nowhere else. The most diverse region on the planet is in the tropical mountains of the Andes. Almost a fifth of the world's plant species are found here. Some of these plants may provide cures in the future for life-threatening illnesses.

What can you do?

What can you do to help preserve the fragile mountains and their irreplaceable treasure house of life? Here are a few ideas:

Saver sense
One of the biggest threats to the mountain environment comes from global warming. As many people believe that this warming is a result of the build-up of carbon dioxide in the atmosphere from burning fossil fuels one way of slowing down the effect would be to cut our consumption of these fuels. In winter, put on an extra layer of clothing instead of turning up the heating. Turn lights off when no one is in a room. Switch appliances such as televisions off properly – don't leave them on stand by. If possible, walk or cycle to school – don't go by car. When you do need to make a longer journey, try to use public transport or arrange lifts with friends. As well as saving mountain wildlife all these things could save your family money. That can't be bad, can it?

Sustainable products
When you go shopping think about who is supplying what you buy and where it comes from. Coffee, for example, is grown in highland regions in various parts of the world, such as those in Brazil, Kenya and Papua New Guinea. Look on the label for signs that the coffee your family buys is sold as a "fair trade" product. This means that the farmers who grew it will get a decent price for their crop. When buying wood products, ask your family to look for signs that the forest where the wood came from is properly managed.

Mountain holidays
If you're lucky enough to take a holiday trip to one of the world's mountain areas, perhaps as a skier or a hiker, take care and keep your impact on the environment to a minimum. Don't cut wood from mountain forests to start campfires. Keep to the trails. It might be fun to go where seemingly no one has gone before but think about the mountain plants you might be trampling underfoot. Snowmobiles might look like fun in winter but they are noisy and polluting, disturbing the wildlife and damaging the environment. Don't leave litter in wild places. Take it home with you and, if possible, pick up any that you see.

The write thing to do!
There are mountains all over the world. Wherever you live the chances are that there will be mountains somewhere not too far away. Find out who is in charge of conservation issues in your country

and find out about organisations that help protect the environment. Write to them and find out what they are doing to help protect mountains. Ask what you can do to help too – and let them know if you're not happy with their answers!

Websites
Here are a few websites for mountain fans to explore:

www.mountainpartnership.org
The Mountain Partnership is a voluntary alliance of partners dedicated to improving the lives of mountain people and protecting mountain environments around the world. The official website of the 2002 Year of the Mountain.

www.mountainvoices.org
Read interviews with hundreds of people from mountain regions all over the world and learn about their lives.

www.mountain.org
An organization dedicated to the preservation of mountain environments and cultures around the world.

www.peopleandplanet.net
A large and fascinating source of information on humans and the planet they live on, including mountains and mountain people.

www.igf.fuw.edu.pl/hill/

A fairly comprehensive listing of mountain and mountain-related websites from around the world.

www.peakbagger.com/cont/worldmap.htm
Start from a map of the world showing the major mountain ranges and begin an exploration of the world's mountains. Includes mountain climbers' descriptions of their climbs.

Glossary

Acclimatization
The process of getting used to, or acclimatized, to the conditions in a particular area.

Algae
Plant-like single-celled organisms that make their own food by converting sunlight to nutrients.

Alpine
Describing high mountain regions generally, or specifically referring to the Alps mountains in Europe.

Biodiversity
The range, or variety, of living things found in a particular place, for example global (world) biodiversity or, on a small scale, the biodiversity of an alpine meadow.

Biome
A very large habitat where living conditions are broadly similar across a wide area, such as the ocean biome, the mountain biome or the desert biome.

Cloud forests
Forests found on tropical mountainsides growing above rainforests at heights of 1,000 metres (3,300 feet) or more; also called elfinwoods as the trees here are smaller than true rainforest trees.

Dew claws
Smaller, inner claws found on the legs of some animals.

Ecosystem
All of the living things in a particular place together with the physical conditions there, such as soil composition and weather, and the ways in which all these things, living and non-living, interact with each other.

Environment
A physical habitat, such as a mountain range, together with all the living things that make their home there.

Erosion
The wearing away of a surface by physical or chemical action.

Extinction
The permanent loss of a type, or species, of living thing from the Earth when the last member of that species has died.

Glacier
A slow-moving river of ice formed by layers of snow piling up over many years in mountains and polar regions.

Global warming
The idea that the overall temperature of the Earth is gradually increasing. Many scientists believe that this is as a result of the greenhouse effect, caused by increased levels of carbon dioxide and other chemicals in the atmosphere that trap heat rising from the Earth's surface.

GPS
This stands for "global positioning system". GPS trackers use signals from a network of satellites to determine an object's position anywhere on Earth. They are widely used by explorers, scientists and the military.

Gullies
Steep-sided narrow ravines cut by water in the sides of mountains.

Habitat
The place where a living thing makes its home. A habitat can be as big as a mountain range or as small as the crack in a boulder.

Hibernation
Entering in to a sleep-like state. Some animals hibernate to survive harsh winter conditions until spring comes and food is plentiful again.

Leeward
The side of something away from the direction of the wind.

Lichen
A partnership between an alga and a fungus, that live together for their mutual benefit.

Migrate
To move from one area to another in search of better living conditions.

Nomad
A member of a tribe of people who have no fixed home but move from place to place, usually in search of pasture for their animals.

Plates
Very large, slow-moving sections of the Earth's crust; movements of the plates are thought to be responsible for the formation of mountain ranges.

Pollinator
Something that carries pollen from one flower to another so that fertilization can take place and seeds can form; the chief pollinators are insects.

Rainshadow
An area in the shadow of a mountain range that receives very little rainfall because moist air is blocked by the mountains.

Refuge
A place of shelter from trouble or danger.

Snowline
The height on a mountain above which temperatures are below freezing and snow does not melt.

Treeline
The height on a mountain above which conditions are too harsh for trees to grow.

Tundra
The cold, treeless region to the south of the north polar regions where the ground is frozen for most or all of the year.

Ultraviolet radiation
High-energy radiation from the sun, invisible to human eyes, that can cause damage to living tissues.

Index